GW00731919

SAN FRANCISCO TRAVEL GUIDE

HUNGRY
PASSPORT

How to use this guide?

SECTIONS ARE DIVIDED BY COLORS

SECTION I

Things to know before you go

Packed with practical info from how to get from the airport to the city, how to get around the city, the best time to visit, the best apps to use, which tours to take, etc.

SECTION II & III

Top 10 attractions & 10 additional ones

The absolute must-see 10 attractions, especially if you are visiting for the first time. If you have more time, find additional impressive landmarks and experiences.

SECTION IV

Itineraries, Day trips, Things to do...

If you don't have the time to plan your own itinerary, you'll find things to do if it's raining, in the winter, in the evening, best day trips, and more.

THIS GUIDE IS INTERACTIVE

Scan the QR code

- **Maps**
- **Tickets**
- **Apps**
- **Info**

TABLE OF CONTENTS

Main MAP

This map includes: Top 20 San Francisco, Best City Views, Interesting Bars and Restaurants, Cheap Eats

Things to Know Before You Go to San Francisco

This section includes:

GENERAL INFO

Facts & Info About San Francisco

Population: 875,114 (2021)
Land area: 47 sq mi (121 km^2)
Best time to visit: Sept.-Nov. (warm temperatures)
For how long: Min. 3 days
Currency: U.S. Dollar - USD ($, US$)

Covid-19 updates

Tourist information

US Visa info

Events Calendar

Drinking Water

Tap water is safe to drink. The water in San Francisco is supposed to be one of the best-tasting tap waters in the U.S. There are water fountains available throughout the city.

Toilets

San Francisco provides self-cleaning toilets across the city. They are also accessible to people with disabilities. You can also use toilets in bars, museums, restaurants, etc.

Safety

Crime info

Overall, San Francisco is a safe city. Some neighborhoods are best to avoid, particularly at night. However, always watch your valuables, and use common sense.

Emergency services number: 911

◄ **Crime rate map**

Type A

Type B

Power Plugs

Power plugs used in the United States are **type A** and **type B**.

Travel Adapters

If you are coming from outside the US, you will need a travel adapter to charge your phone and other devices.

Wheelchair access

Accessibility

San Francisco is a friendly place to people with physical disabilities, including in hotel accommodation, museums, restaurants, etc.

◄ **Wheelchair accessible travel guide**

MONEY

Currency

$ - U.S. Dollar is the official currency of the US and its territories.

$1 is worth approximately:*

€ 0.87 EUR
$ 1.27 CAD
$ 1.39 AUD
£ 0.74 GBP
¥ 116 JPY
₹ 75 INR
$ 20 MXP

Current rates

Data for Jan. 2022

Credit Cards

Most hotels, stores, and restaurants in San Francisco accept major credit cards like Visa or MasterCard.

TIP: It is wise always to have some Dollars in your wallet.

ATMs

There are plenty of ATMs in San Francisco: use Google Maps or a similar app to find one.

WEATHER & CLIMATE

San Francisco has a warm-summer Mediterranean climate with mild but moist winters and dry summers.

Spring

66 °F
19 °C
Average High

Sunny with no rain most of the time.

50 °F - 68 °F
10 °C - 20 °C

Summer

72 °F
22 °C
Average High

Summer is **warm** and **dry**. Often **foggy** & chilly.

55 °F - 72 °F
13 °C - 22 °C

Fall

66 °F
19 °C
Average High

Sunny weather. Mostly with no rain or fog.

50 °F - 68 °F
10 °C - 20 °C

Winter

59 °F
15 °C
Average High

Winter is **mild** & **rainy.** Also dry, sunny periods.

46 °F - 61 °F
8 °C - 16 °C

TRANSPORTATION

From and to San Francisco International Airport (SFO)

San Francisco International Airport is located 13 miles (21 km) south of downtown San Francisco. You can use any of the following means of transportation:

Public Transit ▾

- **BART Rapid Rail**
- **SamTrans Bus Service**
- **Caltrain Commuter Rail**

SFO website

Uber, Lyft

Taxis, Limousines

Shared Ride Vans

Charter Operators

Hotel Shuttles

Car Rentals

Getting around the SFO airport

AirTrain provides 24/7 service with station departures every four minutes

▸ **Red Line:** terminals & garages, BART Station

▸ **Blue Line:** Car rentals, all terminals & garages, BART Station

Arriving by TRAIN

San Francisco Station (4th and King Street/ Caltrain Depot) is a major area transit hub:

- Amtrak & shuttle bus drop-off/pick-up
- BART: Bay Area Rapid Transit

Amtrak

BART

Arriving by CAR

You can use **Google Maps** to get driving directions to San Francisco. Know where to park in advance with apps like Pay by Phone, SpotHero, ParkWhiz and similar (find and book parking locations in the city) - scan the QR code.

Alternatively, you can book one of the many hotels in San Francisco that offer parking.

ParkWhiz

SpotHero

Pay by Phone

Download parking apps

Getting AROUND THE CITY

San Francisco offers plenty of transportation options for getting around the city. Take advantage of Muni (bus and metro system) that runs throughout the city and other types of transportation options:

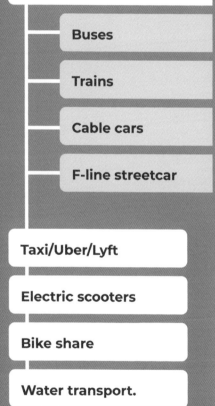

Public transport. MUNI ▾
- Buses
- Trains
- Cable cars
- F-line streetcar

Taxi/Uber/Lyft

Electric scooters

Bike share

Water transport.

Hop on hop off busses

SF MUNI Bus/Rail
Single Ride* **$2.5**
Day Pass **$5**
120 minutes of travel

SF MUNI Cable Car: $7

1-Day, 3-Day and 7-Day Visitor Passport: **$13-47**

IMPORTANT: MUNI Passports are not valid on BART, other transit systems, tour buses, or for transportation to or from airport (SFO).

Use **Muni Mobile** or **Clipper** (The Bay Area transit card)

Muni Mobile

Transit Map

Clipper

ALL LINKS

13

FOOD & DRINKS

We suggest using **Yelp** or **TripAdvisor** to find nearby places with good reviews. Try to avoid sitting down in the restaurants next to major attractions, many times you can find a much better price/quality ratio restaurants a street or two away from the main locations.

AVERAGE PRICES - bars, restaurants

DRINKS

Coffee*	$ 2-4
Water	$ 1-2
Soda	$ 2-3
Beer	$ 5-10
Wine	$ 6-11
Cocktail	$ 5-20

FOOD

Breakfast	$ 5-10
Avg. meal**	$ 10-20+
Pizza slice	$ 4-6
Fast food	$ 6-8
Dungeness crab	$ 20-30

*Coffee at Starbucks or similar: around $5 ** Budget meal: around $10*

Unique Spots

Cheap eats, best bars & more

- Spark Social SF
- Taqueria Cancun
- Red's Java House
- Smuggler's Cove
- Tonga Room & Hurricane Bar, etc.

◄ **See map for more**

ACCOMMODATION

Average hotel price (2 people/night):

from **$150**

TIP 1: The price varies and depends on the location, facilities (level of luxury), etc. Also, pay attention to extra charges like taxes and parking.

TIP 2: You can find better deals if you take the time to research multiple online booking platforms like Airbnb or Booking.

TIP 3: Be flexible with the dates when booking. Try to book accommodation with cancellation options.

BEST AREAS TO STAY

For nightlife: Mission District, SoMa, North Beach

For families: Fisherman's Wharf, Noe Valley

Luxury hotels: Downtown S.F.

LGBTQ neighborhoods: Castro, The Mission

If you are on a budget: Marina District

Cool areas: Haight-Ashbury, Hayes Valley, North Beach, Russian Hill

GOOD TO KNOW

Tipping

You should always tip at restaurants, bars, and hotels and tip taxi drivers in the United States.

The normal rates are:

- **Wait staff at restaurants:**
  Between 15% and 20% pre-tax
- **Bartenders:**
  $1 to $2 per drink OR 15% to 20% of the bar tab

Lines & Crowds

Expect tourists around major attractions. Be prepared to wait in line, reserve tickets in advance, or buy a city pass with skip-the-line privileges.

Internet (Wi-Fi, SIM cards)

Internet

You can purchase a **prepaid SIM card** to access the Internet on your phone. Alternatively, you can consider renting a **pocket WiFi** or mobile hotspot.

The city offers **free WiFi** service in selected places around the city. You can also find WiFi in fast food stores, cafes, restaurants, hotels, etc.

BEST APPS

Restaurants, reviews, make reservations

TripAdvisor Review, book

Yelp Review, find a table

Open Table Book a table

| UberEats | GrubHub |

With locals

Eatwith Eat with locals

Withlocals Tours, etc.

Other apps

Eventbrite Local events

Groupon Coupons

Mr. Chilly Weather app

WiFi Map Find WiFi

Getting around

Google/Apple Maps

| Moovit | Routesy |

Bay Wheels Bikes

Muni Buy tickets

Lime Scooter, bikes

| Uber | Lyft |

Parking

Pay by Phone

SpotHero

Download
these apps

17

City Passes, Tours, Views

City Passes

A great option to save money if you are planning to visit several attractions and want to skip the line at some locations. Check which one suits you best.

Official S.F. CityPASS®

Go San Francisco

S.F. Sight-Seeing Pass

Best City Views

- Coit Tower
- Mission Dolores Park
- The View Lounge
- Alamo Square Park
- Twin Peaks
- Golden Gate Overlook
- Alcatraz Island
- Alta Plaza Park
- Pier 7, etc.

◄ **See map for more**

View MAP for more

City Tours

A great way to discover San Francisco is by a walking tour organized by professional guides who know a great deal about the city's rich history.

Some providers even offer free or **pay-what-you-wish** walking tours. However, at the end of the tour, it is recommended to make a donation (usually between $5 and $20).

Tours are a perfect way to discover the city for tourists who would like to get a sense of the city and those with limited time in San Francisco.

Book your favorite tour

Golden Gate Bridge & Lombard Loop

Chinatown Ghost Walking Tour

San Francisco Bay Sunset Catamaran Cruise

Golden Gate Bridge to Sausalito Bike Tour

Classic Sidecar Tour of San Francisco

Golden Gate Park Segway Tour

Secret Food Tour of Mission District

ABOUT SAN FRANCISCO

San Francisco lies on the West Coast of the United States. It is known as the financial, commercial, and cultural center of Northern California. Steep rolling hills, architecture, food, and world-renowned tourist attractions like cable cars, Golden Gate Bridge, or Alcatraz attract over 25 million visitors each year.

Precolonial history & arrival of Europeans

The evidence of human settlements in the area dates to 3,000 BC. For Native Americans, the bay was a perfect spot for hunting and gathering. In 1769 Spanish explorers were the first Europeans there.

1848 gold rush

The gold rush led to a large population boom, branded by lawlessness, gambling, and prostitution. A growing Asian population also characterized the expansion of the city in the 1800s. Chinatown in San Francisco became the largest Chinese settlement outside of Asia.

The earthquake of 1906

A massive earthquake on April 18, 1906, triggered days-long fires. Entire neighborhoods were destroyed. But the city was quickly rebuilt, eventually becoming one of the major American cities, crowned with the construction of the Golden Gate Bridge in 1933.

The birthplace of the hippie movement

In the 1960s, hippies started gathering in Haight-Ashbury. The counterculture anti-war movement reached its peak with the 1967 Summer of Love.

Tech capital of the world

With the Silicon Valley boom in the late 20th century, San Francisco became one of the world's main tech hubs.

Top 20
MAPS

Top 10 things to do in San Francisco

This section includes:

1

Golden Gate Bridge

· · ·

One of the world's most famous bridges

—

1

ENTRANCE FEE

Free

OPENING HOURS

24/7

Location

Spanning the strait that connects San Francisco Bay with the Pacific Ocean, the Golden Gate Bridge **was the longest suspension bridge** in the world (1.7 mi. or 2.7 km long) when it was constructed in 1937.

Today, it is one of the most famous symbols of the United States and is considered one of the Wonders of the Modern World. With its recognizable vermilion **orange color** and beautiful surroundings, it is also said to be the world's most photographed bridge. The U.S. Navy wanted the bridge painted black & yellow to help passing ships see it fast.

The bridge got its name from the Golden Gate Strait on which it is located (the Golden Gate Strait name comes from **California's gold rush era**).

i **Tip:** Walk or drive across this distinguished landmark to find the best spot for a selfie or even take a boat ride to get under the bridge.

Fisherman's Wharf

· · ·

Iconic waterfront neighborhood

——

2a

Fisherman's Wharf got its name from the fishermen who berthed their boats in the San Francisco wharf and provided food for hordes of **Gold Rush fortune seekers in the 1800s**.

This historic neighborhood has been a world-renowned tourist destination since the 1970s. Among the places of interest in the area are:

- **Pier 39:** Find various shops, restaurants, and other attractions, such as a carousel, an aquarium, the Infinite Mirror Maze, the sea

Location

lions basking on the pier, bay cruises, etc.

- **San Francisco Maritime Nat. Historical Park** with a fleet of historic vessels, a maritime museum, etc.

- **Historic Pier 45:** Here you can see the Vessels from the 2nd World War

- **Madame Tussauds SF:** A wax museum

i **Tip:** Enjoy a meal at Frankie's Pier 43, old-fashioned waterfront counter with outdoor seating.

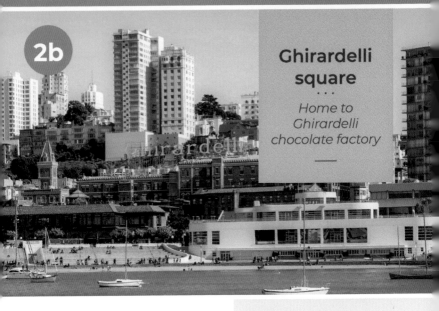

2b

Ghirardelli square

· · ·

Home to Ghirardelli chocolate factory

Location

Rejoice if you are a chocolate lover: you can sample the chocolate squares that made this place famous at the **Ghirardelli chocolate shop** and ice cream store. However, the attractions are usually very crowded, so be ready to line up for a while.

Ghirardelli square stands at one end of Fisherman's Wharf. This well-loved landmark was formerly **a chocolate factory** established by an Italian immigrant.

Today, **Ghirardelli Square** consists of unique shops, award-winning restaurants, and a five-star hotel.

i **Did you know?** Ghirardelli Square is listed on the U.S. National Register of Historic Places.

2b

Theatre program

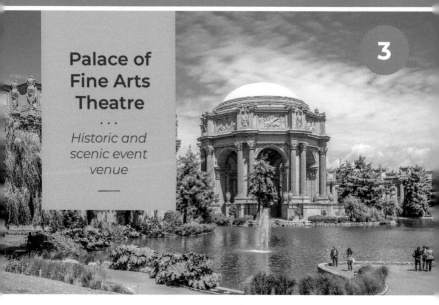

Palace of Fine Arts Theatre

. . .

Historic and scenic event venue

———

ENTRANCE FEE
———
Free

OPENING HOURS

24/7 From outside
For events: Scan the QR code

Location

Palace of Fine Arts was constructed for the **1915 Panama-Pacific International Exposition** to show the world that San Francisco could be rebuilt as an international city after the destructive earthquake and fire of 1906.

In this architectural masterpiece **inspired by Roman ruins**, you'll find a lagoon and walkways, which make it a popular venue for weddings and art exhibitions.

You can also check out the nearby **Wave Organ**, a sculpture that interacts with the waves of the San Francisco Bay. Sit back and relax as you listen to the wave sound effects that vary in intensity based on the tide level.

i **Did you know?** Badly deteriorating rotunda and columns were rebuilt in 1964.

31

Financial District

San Francisco's business hub

—

4

A concentration of high-rise buildings and multinational companies' **corporate headquarters** mark San Francisco's Financial District.

The area went through a construction boom in the latter half of the 20th century because of improved **earthquake-proofing techniques** and lifted building height restrictions.

Visit these attractions:

- **Transamerica Pyramid**: The tallest building before Salesforce Tower.

Location

- **Lotta's Fountain**: A meeting place for survivors of the 1906 earthquake.
- **Jack Kerouac Alley**
- **Maiden Lane:** Pedestrian path with cafes and boutiques .
- **Columbus Tower:** Copper-green building.
- **Chinatown**: The largest outside Asia (see N7).

i **Tip:** Visit Coit tower, Ina Coolbrith Park, or Mission Dolores Park for a perfect view of downtown San Francisco.

Location

Lombard Street

Beautiful Streets

· · ·

Outdoor galleries with murals & vibrant houses

———

5

Rolling hills, stunning ocean views, and pretty streets lined with colorful and cute houses – San Francisco has it all. Explore the following locations (streets):

- **Painted Ladies** near Alamo Square: A row of Victorian and Edwardian houses whose vibrant colors enhance the homes' architectural details.

- **Lombard Street**: A steep one-way street with eight sharp turns, making it "the crookedest street in the world."

- **16th Avenue Tiled Steps**: 163 steps transformed into an artwork through a neighborhood effort.

- **Twin Peaks Blvd**: A scenic lookout located on the road between two hills above SF.

- **Balmy Alley**: Known for its constantly changing collection of murals.

- **Macondray Lane**: A small pedestrian lane.

- **Napier Lane**: Charming alley filled with traditional wooden houses and greenery.

- **Broadway** (the neon-lined stretch near North Beach): A red-light district, known for strip clubs, nightclubs, bars, and more.

Sutro Baths

. . .

Swimming complex in ruins

——

6

ENTRANCE FEE

Free

OPENING HOURS

24/7

Location

Built in the 1890s, the Sutro Baths at Lands End were **formerly the world's largest indoor swimming complex**, with six saltwater pools and one freshwater pool. The baths were unsuccessful because of high maintenance costs. Eventually, the baths got converted into an ice-skating rink in the 1960s. The facility burned down shortly after, leaving the once-glamorous site in ruins.

Don't miss the nearby sea cave and the cave trail that takes you to Point Lobos, Battery Lobos and **Lands End Labyrinth** (Eastern Coastal Trail Overlook).

You can find the **Camera Obscura** just above the baths. It is a large image-projecting device based on Leonardo da Vinci's 15th-century designs. Look through the device for 360-degree live images of the Seal Rocks Area.

i **Tip:** Visit the Baths at sunset for the best view.

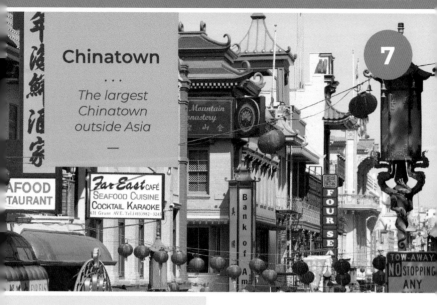

Chinatown

...

The largest Chinatown outside Asia

—

Among the four Chinatowns in San Francisco, the one on Grant Avenue is the **largest outside Asia** and the oldest in North America.

Founded in the mid-19th century, it has played a crucial role among North America's Chinese immigrants. It has kept its language, customs, and identity.

Here you can find several traditional Chinese shops, restaurants and other interesting sights.

Explore the following attractions ▶

Location

- Dragon's Gate
- Sing Chong Building
- Tin How Temple
- Chinese Consolidated Benevolent Association
- Portsmouth Square
- Fortune Cookie factory
- Ross Alley
- China Live market, food emporium, etc.

i **Tip:** If you like interesting neighboorhoods visit also **Japantown** or **Little Italy** full of heritage attractions.

Ferry Building

. . .

The ferry terminal and a food hall

—

8

ENTRANCE FEE

Free

OPENING HOURS

7am - 8pm
Daily

Location

Located on the Embarcadero, the Beaux-Arts style Ferry Building is a terminal for ferries crossing the San Francisco Bay. This landmark, completed in 1898, was the city's largest project at the time of its construction.

It new features a food hall and marketplace where you can buy local and sustainable products. You can get a great view of the **Oakland Bay Bridge** from the building.

Don't miss other attractions in **Central Embarcadero Piers Historic District:**

- Ferry Plaza Farmers Market with local farmers' produce.
- Exploratorium: Museum of science, technology, and arts.
- Pier 7 for fishermen and tourists, for beautiful city views.
- Market Street: A major transit artery.
- Vaillancourt Fountain (Quebec libre!).
- Sue Bierman Park (Ferry Park).
- Pier 33 to go to Alcatraz.

i **Tip:** Join the Ferry Building free tour (QR code).

9

Botanical
Garden

Japanese
Tea Garden

Dutch Windmill

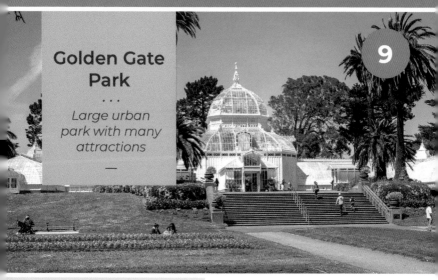

Golden Gate Park

. . .

Large urban park with many attractions

—

9

Golden Gate Park is an urban park stretching across 1,000 acres. It is an ideal place for long walks, picnics, and reading.

Here you can find gardens, meadows, hills, lakes, playgrounds, etc.

Some attractions:

Location

- **S.F. Botanical Garden**: On 55 acres with plants from around the world

- **Bison Paddock** with a herd of American bison

- **Japanese Tea garden**: Oldest public Japanese garden in America

- **Spreckels Lake:** An artificial reservoir

- **Conservatory of Flowers** greenhouse

- **Stow Lake** with Golden Gate Pavilion and Strawberry Hill

- **Dutch and Murphy Windmills**

- **de Young Museum**: A fine arts museum

- **Alvord Lake Bridge**

i **Don't miss:** For sweeping views of the city visit Hamon Observation Tower (entry-free).

Alcatraz Ferry
and Tickets

Alcatraz
Night tour

Alcatraz

. . .

One of the most famous prisons in the World

———

10

ENTRANCE FEE

From $41

OPENING HOURS

9/10am-6pm
Daily

Location

This island is known for the Alcatraz Federal Penitentiary built in the 19ᵗʰ century. The prison was thought to be escape-proof because of strong bay currents and surrounding cold waters. But there were **no confirmed escapes** from the island, except for one prisoner who was found unconscious on the shore. Today, hundreds complete Alcatraz Triathlon, a 1.5 mi./2.4 km annual swim.

The prison became known as "The Rock" and housed more than 1,500 of the most ruthless criminals in America, including **Al Capone**. However, bad reputation and high maintenance costs forced the prison to shut down in 1963.

Alcatraz is open to the public. Make sure to reserve your tickets in advance since they are often sold out.

i **Did you know?** Alcatraz got its name from the Spanish word for *pelican* or *strange bird*?

45

Top 20
MAPS

10 additional things to do in San Francisco

This section includes:

11

Mission
District Tour

Mission District

. . .

San Francisco's art culture and community

—

11

The concentration of street art in the Mission District is one of the highest in the world.

You can view more than 500 murals, created from the 1970s to present day, on alleyways, major streets, large buildings, and even hidden spots.

From these wall paintings, you can gain insights into **socio-political** and **economic issues**, womanhood, Latin American culture, and other themes.

Location

Stroll along the streets of Balmy Alley, Clarion Alley, Cypress, Osage, Caledonia, Horace Alley, Lilac and many others to discover rich street art.

Explore the Mission District on foot to fully appreciate the murals' details.

i **Tip:** If you love interesting neighboorhoods, don't skip vibrant Dogpatch, GLBTQ friendly Castro District, trendy Hayes Valley and Nob Hill with historic mansions.

12

Buy ticket
here

Coit Tower

. . .

*Iconic observation
tower*

___

ENTRANCE FEE
___

$10

OPENING HOURS
___

10am-5pm

Daily

Location

The elegant white concrete column stands in the city's
Pioneer Park, on top of Telegraph Hill. It provides
panoramic views over the bay and the city.

Completed in 1933, the 210-foot Coit Tower gets its name
from wealthy local Lillie Hitchock Coit who left a substan-
tial donation to add this beauty to her beloved city when
she died. In 2008, the tower was added to the National
Register of Historic Places.

Don't miss the **ground-floor murals** depicting life in San
Francisco in the 1930s before heading to the top of the
tower. You can even take a private guided mural tour.

i **Tip:** Visit the tower at sunset for magnificent colors
over the city and the bay.

13

Museums
Websites

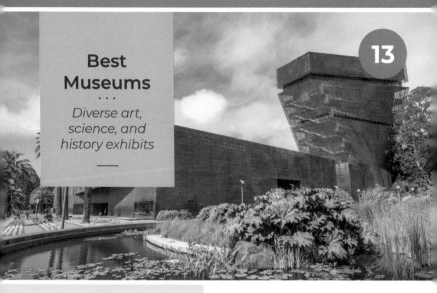

Best Museums
. . .
Diverse art, science, and history exhibits

13

Whether you're an art lover, a science enthusiast, or a history buff, San Francisco has a lot to offer.

Here are some of the city's best museums:

Location

- **de Young Museum:** Fine arts museum
- **California Academy of Sciences:** One of the oldest natural history museums in the world
- **Exploratorium:** Science museum
- **Legion of Honor**: Exhibits a remarkable collection of ancient and European art
- **S.F. Museum of Modern Art** with over 33,000 contemporary paintings, sculptures, etc.
- **The Walt Disney Family Museum**: Walt Disney's life and legacy
- **Wells Fargo Museum:** Depicts Wells Fargo's role in the Gold Rush
- **Musée Mécanique:** Arcade games & artifacts
- **Museum of Craft and Design:** Modern pieces made by local artists
- **Cable Car Museum:** Learn about the San Francisco cable car system history
- **USS Pampanito:** WWII submarine museum
- **Pier 24 Photography**
- **Maritime Museum**

14

Oracle Park
Tickets

Chase Center
Tickets

Oracle Park

. . .

America's most scenic baseball park

———

14

ENTRANCE FEE

Varies
$22 Tours

OPENING HOURS

Varies
Check the website

Location

Situated at the edge of downtown, Oracle Park has been home to the San Francisco Giants since 2000. This **baseball park**, known for its classic design and lovely views, has several other impressive features.

Don't skip the 4K center-field video/scoreboard and the family-friendly Fan Lot. Here you can find a **Giants** memorabilia exhibit, the Wall of Fame, and The Garden, which offers a one-of-a-kind food experience.

In 2004, 122 WiFi access points were installed in Oracle Park, making it one of the World's largest public hotspots at that time.

i **Don't miss:** Chase Center nearby - an indoor arena mainly for basketball with multiple layers and floors. It is home of the Golden State Warriors.

15

Cable Car Tickets

Cable Cars
. . .
An iconic experience in San Francisco
—

15

Beautiful steep hills of San Francisco would not be complete without its traditional cable cars. Ride one of the cable cars that make up the city's cable car system **- the last one of its kind in the World.**

Cable cars in San Francisco were an invention of Andrew Smith Hallidie in 1873. When the masses accepted it as new means of public transportation, it remained the city's primary transportation system for over 30 years.

Three cable car routes:

- **Powell/Hyde**: The most popular one (close to Lombard St, ends at Ghirardelli Square).
- **Powell/Mason**: Close to Lombard st. and drops you off close to Pier 39.

Turnaround

- **California/Van Ness**: Runs through the Financial District.

Part of the city's cable car system is a **turnaround** intersection at Powell and Market Street. The cars are manually turned around before they head back.

San Francisco has many unique-looking **streetcars**. How can you distinguish between the two systems? Both streetcars and cable cars run on steel rails, but streetcars are connected to an overhead wire.

i **Did you know?** San Francisco is home to the world's most diverse collections of trams in regular service.

Theatre District

. . .

Neighborhood with many theatres

—

The San Francisco Theatre District is named for the authentic theaters and impressive collection of unique venues located in this neighborhood.

If you like **shows** and performances, explore one of the following **theatres**: Orpheum Theatre (Orpheum Theatre), S.F. Playhouse, Golden Gate Theatre, Curran Theatre.

Visit also Civic center plaza (see N20) and Union Square shopping district with the Goddess of Victory statue in the middle.

Location

The plaza was built in 1850 and boasts San Francisco's largest collection of department stores and luxury boutiques.

If you visit in the winter, don't skip **Winter Walk** offering food trucks, family-friendly activities, performances, etc.

i **Don't miss:** Shows & perfomances (scan the QR code).

17

Haight-Ashbury

. . .

Birthplace of the 1960s hippie movement

—

17

Haight-Ashbury, named after two streets, is known as the **birthplace of the 1960s hippie counterculture**.

This neighborhood with rich history is also famous for its **colorful murals** and **Victorian-style homes**. In fact, it has the highest concentration of Victorian houses in San Francisco. In the Haight (as the locals call it), you can shop at one of many vintage stores or watch a free show at the largest independent music store in the World.

Hike to the top of **Buena Vista Park** for amazing city and bay views.

Location

i **Don't skip:** Piedmont Boutique, a costume store with a giant pair of legs sticking out of the window.

Fort Mason
Center

Off the Grid
Events

Fort Mason Center

. . .

Center for arts and culture

—

18

ENTRANCE FEE

Free

OPENING HOURS

6³⁰am-12am
Daily

Location

This waterfront complex of **renovated military buildings** hosts an ever-changing lineup of artistic programs, including dance and theater performances, art exhibits, cultural classes, and culinary events.

Visit the center's parking lot on Friday evening to experience **Off the Grid**, a free-admission extravaganza of food trucks and music by emerging artists. Enjoy gourmet food in open-air dining areas with lounges and firepits.

Considered to be the leader of the **mobile food movement**, you will find Off the Grid at other interesting locations in San Francisco.

i **Tip:** Check for the culural events (scan the QR code).

19

Andy Goldsworthy's Wood Line

Presidio
Website

Presidio

. . .

*1,500-acre park
on a former
military post*

—

19

This former military post is a major outdoor recreation area with forests, miles of hiking trails, scenic overlooks and even a golf course.

Location

Don't miss the following attractions:

- **Fort Point National Historic Site:** A masonry seacoast fortification.
- **Battery Boutelle:** A reinforced concrete coastal gun battery on Fort Winfield Scott
- **Walt Disney Family Museum:** Life and legacy of Walt Disney
- **Battery Chamberlin:** Historic coastal defense site
- **SF National Cemetery:** A military cemetery
- **Torpedo Wharf**

- **Marshall's and Baker Beach**
- **Mountain Lake**: One of the city's last surviving natural lakes
- **Lyon Street Steps**
- **Off the grid**: Presidio Picnic
- **Andy Goldsworthy's Wood Line**
- **Batteries to Bluffs Trail:** Footpath along the coastline, offering cliff and ocean views
- **Crissy Field Marsh**

i **Did you know?** Presidio was established as Spain's outpost in the Americas in 1776.

Civic Center Plaza

. . .

Home to S.F. City Hall

—

20

Civic Center Plaza a.k.a. Joseph Alioto Piazza is a large plaza located in Civic Center.

After the city was selected to **host the 1915 Panama-Pacific International Exposition**, numerous public improvements were proposed in San Francisco, including the City Hall design competition. The Plaza is almost symmetrical from north to south.

There have been multiple reconstructions in the square since it was established over one hundred years ago.

Location

Don't miss the following attractions around the Plaza:

- San Francisco City Hall
- S.F. Public Library
- Asian Art Museum
- Herbst Theatre
- War Memorial Opera House
- Heart of the City Farmers' Market

i **Tip:** Visit also other beautiful squares like Alamo Square, St. Mary's Square, Washington Square, etc.

Itineraries, Things to Do, Best Day Trips

This section includes:

ITINERARIES

To make your trip to San Francisco stress-free and organized, we prepared simple one, two, and three-day itineraries. Each suggested itinerary includes a dedicated QR code to a customized Google Map that you can easily use on your phone.

 ◄ MAP

1-Day Itinerary

Morning

- Presidio: Fort Point National Historic Site if time
- Golden Gate Bridge
- The Palace Of Fine Arts
- Fisherman's Wharf: Ghirardelli, Pier 45 (if time), Pier 39, etc.
- Powell/Mason Cable Car Turnaround - if time

Afternoon & Evening

- Lombard Street
- Coit Tower: view towards the Financial District and the bay
- Embarcadero: Ferry Building
- Financial District: Transamerica & Redwood Park
- Chinatown
- Night out: explore Valencia Street and the rest of Mission District

2-Day Itinerary

MAP ▸

Day 1

Morning

- Presidio: Fort Point National Historic Site if time
- Golden Gate Bridge
- The Palace Of Fine Arts
- Cable Car turnaround
- Fisherman's Wharf

Afternoon

- Lombard Street
- Coit Tower: view towards the Financial District and the bay
- Embarcadero: Ferry Building
- Financial District
- Chinatown

Evening

- See a show OR
- Night out: explore Valencia Street, Mission District

Day 2

Morning

- Lands End Labyrinth - if time
- Sutro Baths
- Camera Obscura & Holograph - if time
- Golden Gate park: Dutch Windmill, Stow Lake, S.F. Botanical Garden, de Young Museum, Japanese Tea Garden, Conservatory of Flowers, etc.

Afternoon & Evening

- Haight-Ashbury
- Painted Ladies
- Buena Vista Park

Evening

- Off the grid at Fort Mason Center
- Night out in town

◄ MAP

3-Day Itinerary

Day 1

Morning

- Presidio: Fort Point National Historic Site - if time
- Golden Gate Bridge
- Palace Of Fine Arts
- The Wave Organ

Afternoon & Evening

- Fisherman's Wharf: Ghirardelli, Pier 39, Historic Pier 45, etc.
- Cable Car turnaround
- Lombard Street
- Japan Town - if time
- See a show OR explore unique bars

Day 2

Morning

- Alcatraz Island

Day 2 - continue

Afternoon & Evening

- Coit Tower - if time
- Embarcadero: Exploratorium, Ferry Building, etc.
- Chinatown
- Little Italy (if time)
- Off the grid at Fort Mason Center OR night out in town

Day 3

Morning

- Lands End Labyrinth
- Sutro Baths
- Camera Obscura
- Golden Gate park

Afternoon & Evening

- Haight-Ashbury
- Buena Vista Park
- Painted Ladies
- Explore Mission Dist.

Best Day Trips

BOOK
A TOUR ▸

Monterey and Carmel

Drive down the California's scenic Highway 1 to the charming coastal cities where you will have time to explore different attractions and go shopping.

Napa and Sonoma Valley

Learn about Napa and Sonoma's renowned wine culture. Visit top wineries, sample vintage wines with a leisure lunch, & view stunning vineyard-covered hills.

Muir Woods and Sausalito

Muir Woods National Monument Park is famous for its 1000-year-old redwoods. Sausalito is a seaside town, home to a historic houseboat community.

Yosemite

This UNESCO World Heritage Site is located in the Sierra Nevada mountains. It is known for cliffs, waterfalls, sequoia trees and plenty of wildlife.

Silicon Valley

Home to headquarters of the world's biggest companies, such as YouTube, Uber, Twitter, Facebook and Google visitors' centers, Computer History Museum.

All activities
& links

Things to do...

...IN THE SUMMER

- Enjoy some food at Spark Social SF or District Six
- Attend festivals and other events
- Enjoy some food at Off the grid
- Embark on a whale or walking tour
- Chill out in one of many rooftop bars, like Charmaine's Rooftop Bar & Lounge
- Visit farmers market like Heart of the City
- Outdoor activities, like surfing, sailing or paddleboarding
- Outdoor theater
- Explore green areas Bot. Garden, Mission Dolores Park

...IN THE WINTER

- Try ice skating at Holiday Ice Rink
- Attend Christmas markets, like Winter Park at Civic Center
- Explore Ferry Building and Ferry Plaza Farmers Market
- Go shopping at Westfield SF Centre
- Discover unique bars, coffee shops and bakeries, like Tartine Bakery
- Walk around Farmers' Market at Crocker Galleria
- Enjoy some sports and other games at Chase Center
- Visit museums
- Go to the Aquarium

Things to do...

...IF IT'S RAINING

- Explore Ferry Plaza Farmers Market
- Unique bars, coffee shops, and bakeries, like The Interval at Long Now
- Visit aquarium
- Go shopping at Anchorage Square
- Try some food at State Bird Provisions
- Enjoy sports events at Chase Center
- Visit Ferry Plaza Farmer's Market
- Miniature Golf
- The SF Dungeon
- Conservatory of Flowers
- Visit museums

...IN THE EVENING

- Explore quirky bars, cocktail lounges, and breweries, like Smuggler's Cove, Whitechapel, Alchemist, Black Hammer Brewing
- Go clubbing at DNA Lounge, Raven Bar, Temple or Monarch
- Explore North Beach, Mission District, Dogpatch
- Dining experiences, like Foreign Cinema
- Miniature Golf
- Enjoy some shows in a Theatre District
- Embark on a sunset cruise, Alcatraz or other night tour
- Admire Bay Bridge

All activities
& links

San Francisco Travel Guide by Hungry Passport
4225 Solano Ave. Ste 63, Napa CA 94558, USA

www.hungrypassport.xyz

Disclaimer: While we do our best to provide the most current information, opening hours change on a regular basis, businesses close, etc. so we do not guarantee any information in this travel guide is accurate. If you are in doubt, always research on your own. We are not endorsed by any business or other entity presented in this guide.

Printed in Great Britain
by Amazon